# Leadership Theory 101

How to take complex leadership theories and apply them

Randy Wheeler, MA

*Copyright © 2022 by Wheeler Coaching Systems, LLC*

*All rights reserved. This book or any portion thereof may not be reproduced or used in any manner whatsoever without the express written permission of the publisher except for the use of brief quotations in a book review.*

*Although every precaution has been taken to verify the accuracy of the information contained herein, the author and publisher assume no responsibility for any errors or omissions. No liability is assumed for damages that may result from the use of information contained within.*

*Printed in the United States of America*

*First Printing, 2022*

ISBN:
ISBN-

## DEDICATION

This is dedicated to those who have been through the struggle of growth that comes through learning so you can become better at what you do.

# ACKNOWLEDGMENTS

I'd like to acknowledge the professors at Indiana Wesleyan University who first introduced me to these concepts during the course of my Master in Organizational Leadership study. Without their wisdom this would not have been possible.

# Table of Contents

1. Trait Approach
2. Skills Approach
3. Style Approach
4. Situational Leadership Approach
5. Contingency Theory
6. Path-Goal Theory
7. Leader-Member Exchange Theory
8. Transformational Leadership
9. Authentic Leadership
10. Team Leadership
11. Psychodynamic Approach

# Introduction

When I earned my Masters in Organizational Leadership I had the opportunity to study multiple theories of leadership. Although much of what I do centers around the idea of transformational leadership, this resource was created during my educational experience to provide the foundational principles of major leadership theories. Each theory is defined, and a model provided where applicable. Key terms and definitions are provided as necessary for understanding the theory. I originally designed this to apply to those who coach athletes but have also added implications for those in business. Whenever possible I have provided a practical action step or steps to help apply the theory. Each approach, theory, or model has the name of an assessment commonly used to help leaders improve their self-awareness in relationship to the leadership model and/or to assist others in doing the same.

Although this handbook was originally designed for those leading athletes, the resource is useful for all leaders. Leaders in any industry often function like a sport coach providing expert advice (not to be confused with the leadership coaching I do which helps others think into their results). Similarly, all sport coaches, regardless of title, are leaders. Leadership can be developed through continual growth. I hope you find this both an educational and practical resource as you read it.

Randy Wheeler, MA

# Trait Approach

Are leaders born? Is leadership a genetic trait endowed to a select few? Well, yes, I haven't met a leader who was not born, how about you? There may be some individuals who have a natural tendency toward leading.

Think back to your school days, was there one kid who always seemed to have others following him or her whether toward good or bad outcomes? Maybe you were that kid. These are the individuals that theorists would argue have natural leadership traits.

Although thinking has evolved over time and people now understand leadership skills can be developed, this theory provides language to key traits for effective leadership. Some people demonstrate them naturally while others must develop them.

**Definition:**

Trait approach looks at leadership from the leader's point of view. The overall concept is that certain people are born to be leaders because of the traits they possess. Leadership is based on having certain personality characteristics.

Trait theory seeks to explain what qualities create great leaders. Peter Northouse identified researchers such as Stogdill, Mann, Kirkpatrick, Locke and others who have created lists totaling over 30 traits (Northouse, 2010). Through evaluating the research, five major traits arose as the most important traits a leader should have. The following traits: intelligence, self-confidence, determination, integrity, and sociability are described more in detail in the following section (Northouse, 2010).

Northouse describes the "Five-Factor Personality Model" which defines five personality traits that Northouse said Judge and colleagues (2002) found have "a strong relationship" to "being an effective leader" (Northouse, 2010, p. 22). The following factors which are described in the next section are: *neuroticism, extraversion, openness, agreeableness, and conscientiousness* (Northouse, 2010).

One of the most recent concepts addressed in the trait approach is "emotional intelligence" which Northouse explains has been explored by researchers such as Mayer, Salovey, and Caruso and made most familiar to leaders by Daniel Goleman (Northouse, 2010). This concept is the ability for a person to understand intellectually what is occurring emotionally. For example, the individual who experiences intense frustration with a follower and pauses to understand this emotion instead of releasing the emotion in a possibly destructive manner.

**Terms:** (Northhouse, 2010)

*Intelligence* – strong perceptual and verbal abilities and reasoning

*Self-Confidence* – certainty about one's skills and competence

*Determination* - being proactive, having drive, can be dominant, persistent and has initiative

*Integrity* – actions match with words

*Sociability* – friendliness, diplomacy, tact, outgoing, and courteous

*Neuroticism* – traits of anxiety, insecurity, vulnerable, depressed and hostile

*Extraversion* – outgoing in a very positive manner

*Openness* – creative, insightful, curious, informed

*Agreeableness* – conforms, trusts, accepting, and nurtures

*Conscientiousness* – organized, controlled, dependable, thorough, and decisive

**Implications:**

Looking for the top five traits in your athletes, assistant coaches, leadership team or employees will equip a leader to identify their up and coming leaders to develop.

If an athlete/coach/leader lacks one of the traits, the leader may want to evaluate how influential a role they are given.

If the organizational leader or head coach is lacking some of the traits or more importantly the five major traits, then he should seek ways to grow.

If a leader is looking for these traits in others, he should be modeling them himself.

If character/integrity is lacking, be slow to provide the individual with leadership responsibilities.

**Putting it in action:**

Create drills that take your players out of their comfort zone where they must demonstrate these traits and observe. Do they do the drill correct, with passion, confidently? Do they help their teammates? If the coach isn't watching, are they still working at the same level? What do the coaches do in these situations?

Provide assignments for those you lead where they are out of their comfort zone. Observe how they respond to the assignment. What natural abilities arise? If you see any of the top five traits in some of the individuals you lead, how can you help them continue to develop as leaders?

**Assessment Tool:**

*Leadership Trait Questionnaire (LTQ)*

A tool that assesses one's leadership characteristics. LTQ looks at an individual's traits and helps them find their strong and weak areas. This could help a leader determine where the coach/player would fit best on the team or in the organization (Northouse, 2010).

# Skills Approach

Have you ever been in an organization where an individual who was a great technician got promoted . . . and flopped? Maybe they were a star salesperson, but when they became a sales manager, they struggled. Possibly they were a great athlete or technician in their craft, but when they were put in a position to lead others they greatly underperformed.

What causes this? We all have various specific and general skills but depending on the position we fulfill on a team or in an organization some of them may be underdeveloped. The more one moves up in an organization the greater the need for certain abstract skills that help with developing relationships and strategies. This theory helps us understand those skills and to what degree we should be utilizing them based on our position on the team or in the organization.

**Definition:**

This theory evaluates leadership from the leader's perspective. Certain knowledge and abilities are necessary for effective leadership. Northouse describes Katz's three skills needed for leadership: technical, human and conceptual (Northouse, 2010 citing Katz, 1955). The leader's position determines how much of each skill is needed. As illustrated in Figure 1, a lower-level position requires more technical skill while a top-level position requires more conceptual (abstract thinking) abilities. All three levels require equal levels of ability to work with people (Katz, 1955).

Mumford and colleagues developed the "Skills Model" which highlights certain competencies and attributes that lead to effective problem solving and performance (Northouse, 2010 citing Mumford, et al., 2000, p.12). These competencies are:

- Problem solving
- Social judgment – the ability to understand people and social dynamics
- Knowledge – the ability to gather and organize information. (Figure 2)

Four attributes (or "individual approach" in Figure 2) impact leadership competencies:

1. General cognitive ability – intelligence

2. Crystallized cognitive ability – learned intellectual ability

3. Motivation – the leader's willingness to advance the organization's cause

4. Personality.

These attributes and competencies combine to influence a leader's performance and effectively solve complex organizational problems. (Northouse, 2010, pp. 39 – 53).

Figure 1

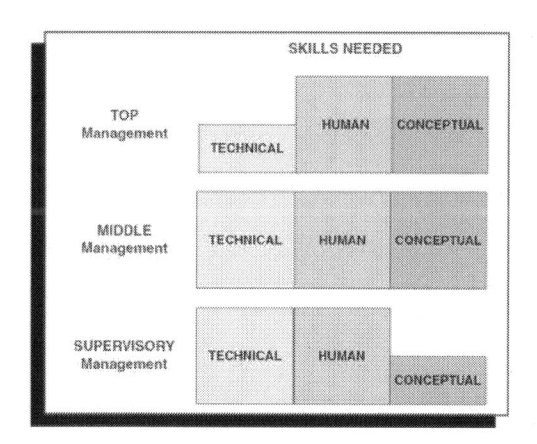

http://3.bp.blogspot.com/_d5n8ghzut5g/SYd8GGY1wII/AAAAAAAAAIk/a3o_ze4lGF0/s400/katz2.png

Figure 2

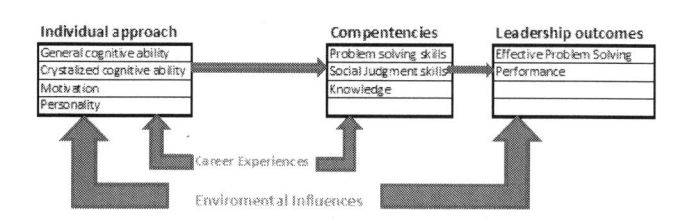

http://www.abolrous.com/hazem/images/Leadership/mhtAAC0(1).png

**Implications:**

Coaches and organizational leaders need to have technical, human, and conceptual skills. As one leads at higher levels such as head assistant/manager/VP or head coach/C-suite/owner, the human and conceptual become more critical because they must have a clear vision and understand the organization or team from the highest level possible. The higher the position the more valuable conceptualizing the future becomes.

Developing athletes/employees into leaders requires helping them learn problem solving skills.

Knowing how to execute the sport or skill is not good enough, as a coach one must be able to relate the concepts in a manner that is applicable.

Be vigilant in helping athletes/employees learn the key competencies of problem solving, social judgment, and knowledge.

**Putting it in action:**

Use athlete/technician, assistant coach/manager mistakes as opportunities for teaching how to solve problems better and make better choices.

Use classroom time/development time to help athletes/employees develop habits that assist in the ability to accumulate and organize information.

As you promote a person out of a technical role or have a new leader, take time to come alongside them and help them with developing big picture (conceptual) thinking and if needed relational skills.

If you are in a business role evaluate how much time you spend in the areas of technical, human, and conceptual thought. Does your division of time align with where you should be based on your role? If not, what do you need to do differently?

Have those you lead evaluate if they are spending the appropriate amount of time on technical, human, and conceptual thinking.

**Assessment Tool:**

*Skills Inventory*

This assessment tool helps determine individual leadership skills and individual strengths and weaknesses. The skills inventory is designed to be a "self-instruction" tool (Northouse, 2010, p.63).

# Style Approach

Have you ever worked on a project with a group and someone in the group drives the group to get the work done? On that same team was there someone who kept the mood light and made sure the people in the group were taken care of? These are two different styles.

In my work with teams and organizations I utilize an assessment that looks deeper at this idea of task versus relationship focus. Everyone has natural tendencies toward one over the other. I could go deeper, but just contact me at randy@wheelercoachingsystems.com and we can talk about how to help you and your organization better understand human behavior and more effective communication.

This theory provides language to see where we fall in our leadership approach in relation to task and relationships. As you will see it may not be distinctly one over the other, but instead we lead in a range of different approaches.

**Definition:**

This approach looks at leadership from the leader's perspective and examines the leader's behavior. Northouse describes the two most recognized studies that influenced this approach: *The Ohio State Studies* and *The University of Michigan Studies* (Northouse, 2010, pp. 70-71). Each study uses different terms but came to the same conclusion: *a leader either focuses his or her style on accomplishing a task or focuses on the relationships with followers to accomplish goals.*

Blake and Mouton furthered the language of this approach by creating the Leadership Grid (Figure 3) which describes five styles of leading that are more clearly defined in the next section: country-club, team, middle-of-the-road, impoverished, and authority-compliance management. This grid expands on the relationship versus task perspective by providing language for various degrees of relationship or task focus.

*Leadership Grid Style Definitions:*

- *Authority-compliance* – heavy emphasis on task, low on people
- *Country-club management* – heavy on relationships, low on task
- *Impoverished management* – unconcerned about task or relationships
- *Middle-of-the-Road management* – compromisers, keeps peace

- *Team management* – emphasizes both task and people

Figure 3

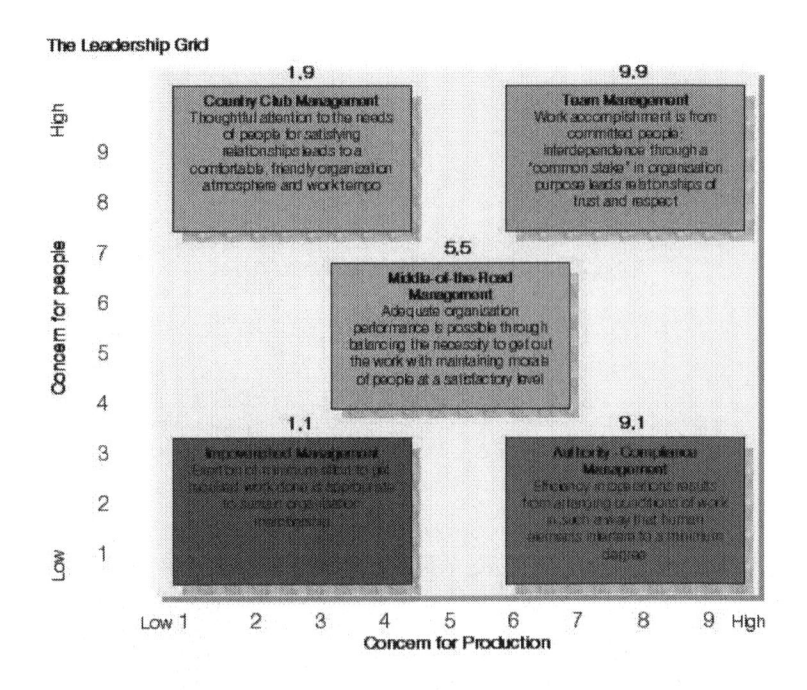

**The Leadership Grid**

| | Low Concern for Production | High Concern for Production |
|---|---|---|
| **High Concern for people (1,9)** | Country Club Management: Thoughtful attention to the needs of people for satisfying relationships leads to a comfortable, friendly organization atmosphere and work tempo | **(9,9)** Team Management: Work accomplishment is from committed people; interdependence through a "common stake" in organization purpose leads relationships of trust and respect |
| **Middle (5,5)** | | Middle-of-the-Road Management: Adequate organization performance is possible through balancing the necessity to get out the work with maintaining morals of people at a satisfactory level |
| **Low Concern for people (1,1)** | Impoverished Management: Exertion of minimum effort to get required work done is appropriate to sustain organization membership | **(9,1)** Authority - Compliance Management: Efficiency in operations results from arranging conditions of work in such a way that human elements interfere to a minimum degree |

http://www.coachingcosmos.com/resources/Leadership+grid+2.jpg

**Implications:**

A coach/leader should know his natural style.

Successful coaches/captains/leaders/managers balance task and relationship well.

Beware of using coercion over influence.

Look for what your players/employees natural tendencies are: task or relationship?

**Putting it in action:**

Use team building drills to put athletes in situations where they demonstrate task and relationship value.

Examples:

1. Get your team through a "spider web" without using the same hole twice or touching the sides.

2. Get your team over a 10-foot-tall wall and everyone can only go one time.

3. Any activity that forces the team to solve a problem and provides an opportunity to see tendencies to focus on people or task

Engage in an assessment such as the Maxwell DISC Personality Indicator* to get an objective assessment of individual preference for task and relationship and use the results to help improve communication in business-related projects.

Observe interactions in a project meeting to assess leadership strengths related to task and relationships.

**Assessment Tools:**

*Style Questionnaire*

Common tools are the "Leader Behavior Description Questionnaire" (LBDQ) (Northouse citing Stogdill, 1963) and the Leadership Grid discussed previously. Both provide the test taker with information to clarify if they tend to be relationship or task oriented. The Style Questionnaire is a simplified version of these tests to help one discern their personal leadership style in relation to task and relationships.

*The Maxwell DISC Personality Indicator\** – helps individuals understand their personal communication style and preferences toward tasks and relationships to help improve their connecting ability with others. This also includes the POWER DISC which evaluates your leadership strengths in seven specific areas.


\*Contact me at randy@wheelercoachingsystems.com to find out more about this tool and others like it or go to https://bit.ly/disclead to invest in one and better understand your style.

# Situational Leadership Approach

Life is complicated and no one theory works for everyone. People are complicated and need varying approaches of leadership depending on their situation. When I was a strength and conditioning coach I learned to modify my approach based on the individual's maturity, experience, and talents.

When new athletes entered the weight room everyone would start with the same fundamental instruction. After setting the expectation in the first few sessions I would then modify my approach based on their individual needs. Some individuals progressed quicker due to their ability and competence while others went at a slower progression.

At times I had individuals who wanted their workouts more specialized. If they had proven their commitment to the process and were competent in the fundamental skills I would adjust their workouts to create a more specialized experience. Little did I realize at the time I was incorporating the situational leadership approach which is the topic of this section.

**Definition:**

This approach looks at leadership from the standpoint of leadership style in relation to situations and the subordinate's commitment and competence. (Figure 4) A leader matches their style to the competence and commitment of his or her followers.

As both grow the leader decreases his or her directive behaviors and increases supportive influence. The leader adjusts his or her style based on the development level of the subordinate as illustrated in Figure 4 (Northouse, 2010).

The model is more easily understood by dividing it into two parts "leadership style" and "development level of subordinates" (Northouse, 2010, p.90). This approach defines styles as "the behavior pattern of a person who attempts to influence others" and involves both task and relationship "behaviors" (Northouse, 2010, p. 91). The next section describes more in detail the four primary styles used by this approach: directing, coaching, supporting, and delegating.

The leader matches his or her style with the development level of the follower. This model provides four development levels that are outlined in the chart below. According to Blanchard the development level is the degree of competence and commitment the subordinates have in relation to the task they are attempting to accomplish (Northouse, 2010 citing Blanchard et. al., 1985). This is an extremely practical approach to leadership that is explained and illustrated (Fig. 4) more in detail below.

**Styles Defined** (Blanchard et al., 1985):

*Directing* – the leaders focuses on achieving goal(s) and clearly informs the follower how to accomplish the goal. The leader is very involved at this level.

*Coaching* – the leader encourages and involves the follower in making decisions

*Supporting* – the follower has control of daily decisions and the leader is available for support and feedback

*Delegating* – the leader gives the follower the objective and has him or her accomplish the job how he or she sees fit

Follower Development Levels (Blanchard et al., 1985):

| Development Level | Competence | Commitment |
| --- | --- | --- |
| D1 | Low | High |
| D2 | Some | Low |
| D3 | Moderate to High | Moderate |
| D4 | High | High |

**Implications:**

This is an excellent model for mentoring younger coaches/new employees and knowing when to give them increased responsibility. The greater the competence and commitment, the more responsibility they can handle.

Coaches/leaders naturally work through these stages as players/employees develop from rookies to veterans.

As coaches are aware of an athlete's or an assistant's developmental level, they can adjust how much responsibility or freedom they provide.

Key questions to ask in understanding situations:

What is the task?

How complex is the task?

Does the individual have skills to accomplish the task?

Does the individual have the desire to complete the job once it begins?

**Putting it in action:**

Help those you lead understand the basics of this concept through teaching them as well as modeling the approaches to begin them on the path toward effective leadership.

In business evaluate those you directly lead and determine if they need clear direction, supportive encouragement, coaching to help them learn, or empowerment with a project they lead.

**Assessment Tool:**

*Situational leadership questionnaire*

This tool provides the individual with work situations and options of what style to use for the given situation. The questionnaire may have the individual determine the follower's development level and decide what approach to use based on the situation. Through their assessment the individual learns his or her "primary and secondary leadership styles, their flexibility, and their leadership effectiveness" (Northouse, 2010, p. 103).

NOTE: A visual model of this theory can be seen on the next page in Fig. 4

Figure 4

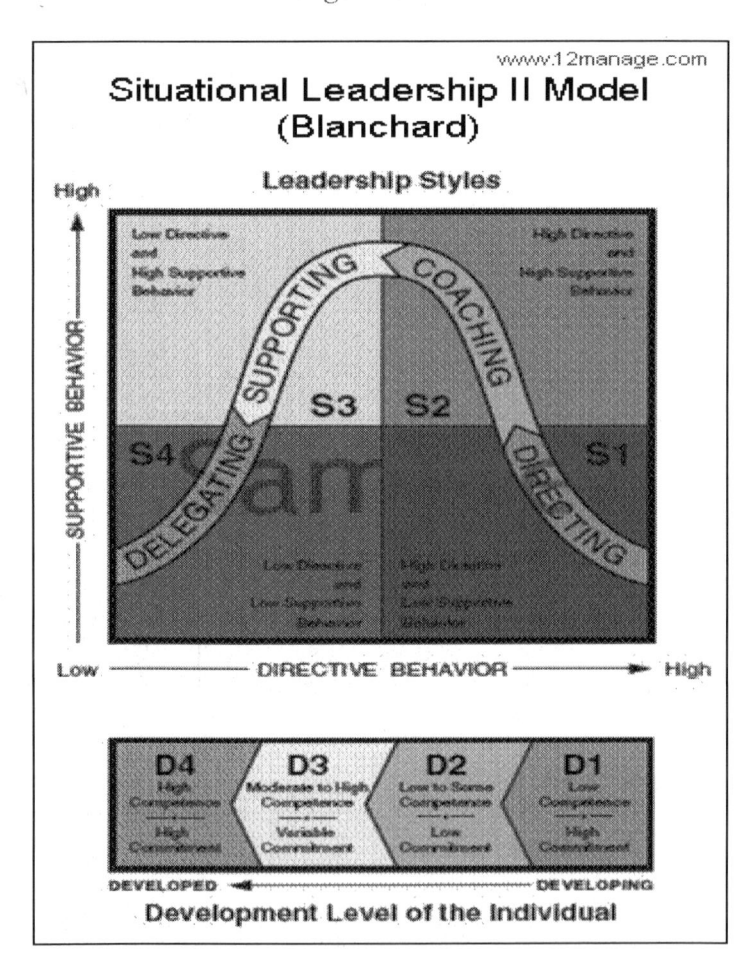

http://www.12manage.com/images/picture_blanchard_situational_leadership.gif

# Contingency Theory

Have you had a leader or a coach who falls apart under stress while another leader seems to excel in the chaos? I spent years among various sport coaches. Each coach had a different style they unknowingly used in their approach to leading.

Coaching a sports team can be quite stressful at times especially if your job security is contingent on the results. I have been around coaches who under pressure become extremely focused on the task of winning and can come across as uncaring. On the other hand, I have seen coaches who under stress become greater encouragers.

The relational leaders thrive in situations where the game is within control while the task-oriented leaders thrive under the pressure of trying to regain control. This theory helps leaders understand where they fall. How does you style impact your relationships? What kind of influence or buy-in do you have from those you lead? Are you effectively using your position of leadership in a way that wins people to you or pushes them away?

**Definition:**

This theory matches leaders to specific situations. The leader's effectiveness is based on how their style fits the situation. The styles are approached from either a task orientation or a relationship orientation (Northouse, 2010).

Three situational variables exist which are defined more in detail in the next section: "leader-member relations, task structure, and position power" (Northouse, 2010, p.112) . As can be seen in Figure 5 each area is evaluated in a different manner.

A leader assesses their "preferred leadership style" through a scale Fiedler (1967) developed called the "Least Preferred Coworker (LPC) scale" (Northouse, 2010, p.112). This scale determines how a leader's task or relationship orientation (High or Low LPC) will interact with the working situation.

Low LPC individuals are task motivated and are best in situations that are either going smoothly or out of control. High LPC individuals are relationship motivated and are effective when there is some certainty and moderate control of the situation (Northouse, 2010). As an individual leader understands their style it helps them to be more appropriately matched to the correct situation.

**Terms:**

*Leader-member relations* – defines the amount of loyalty, confidence and attraction followers feel for leader

*Measurement* – Good or Poor

*Task structure* – defines the clarity of the task requirements

*Measurement* – Structured/High or Unstructured/Low

*Position power* – defines the authority the leader has to punish or reward

*Measurement* – Strong or Weak

**Implications:**

Understanding if those you lead are task or relationship oriented will help in effectively motivating them.

Give leaders enough position power to effectively fulfill role/task.

The LPC test can be used to assess your team's view of you which reveals where you need to adjust your style.

Understand your tendency (task or relationship) and adjust your leadership to meet those with a different tendency. Example: You are task oriented – be aware of when you need to be more relationally in tune.

If your style is not appropriate for the situation, adjust.

**Putting it in action:**

Create team building activities that help you understand your players. Put them in challenging physical situations to find your task people (the people who tell others to "shut-up" and get it done) and your relationship people (the people who are watching over teammates and encouraging them even when it is hard).

In business evaluate your natural leadership tendencies. In what ways do you need to adjust your tendencies so others respond better?

Corporate team building exercises are a great way to understand your employees whether done off-site or on-site.

**Assessment Tool:**

Least Preferred Coworker (LPC) Measure

This tool determines if an individual is task motivated, relationship motivated or independent by describing a co-worker that was difficult to work with. The results provide a score of Low (task), Middle (independent), or High (relationship) LPC to help an individual determine his or her style (Northouse, 2010).

Figure 5

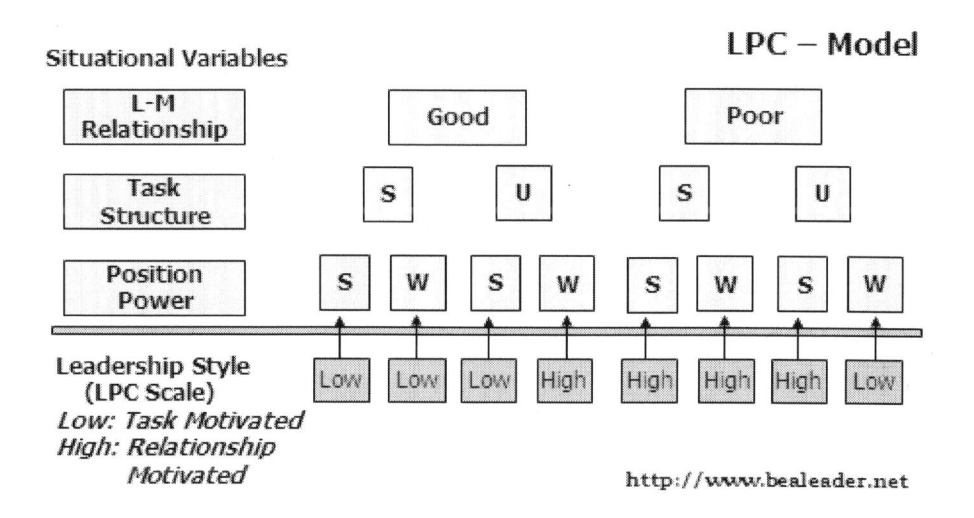

| Situational Variables | | | | | | | | | LPC – Model | |
|---|---|---|---|---|---|---|---|---|---|---|
| L-M Relationship | | Good | | | | Poor | | | | |
| Task Structure | | S | | U | | S | | U | | |
| Position Power | S | W | S | W | S | W | S | W | | |
| Leadership Style (LPC Scale) | Low | Low | Low | High | High | High | High | Low | | |

*Low: Task Motivated*
*High: Relationship Motivated*

http://www.bealeader.net

http://www.bealeader.net/images/lpc-model.png

35

# Path-Goal Theory

As we discussed in situational leadership, determining how to approach a person in a conversation is the art of leadership. This art can be methodical at times though. I think of working with athletes that you have for a four-year period.

In the beginning your leadership will be very directive because you want them to clearly understand what the norms and expectations are of your team. After a year the relationship evolves, and the athlete and coach work together to help new athletes understand the team's culture.

Over time this evolution continues, and the coach challenges his or her athletes to take charge of the team and be the driving force behind clarifying and living out the expectations. This is the ideal, but as you will see below, leaders can make the process more difficult when expectations are confusing or unclear.

If you have been leading a team for any period of time, then you are probably implementing this strategy. As you work through this section evaluate if you are unintentionally creating obstacles to effectively lead others. Also, think through those you lead and determine if you are utilizing the most beneficial leadership style.

**Definition:**

This theory defines how leaders help followers overcome obstacles to help them reach their goals. Three criteria are considered in this theory: leadership style, subordinates traits, and work environment (Northouse, 2010). The leader provides followers with the information, skills, or incentives they need to reach their goals. Figure 6 illustrates the components of this theory.

Like Situational Leadership, leaders adapt their style to the situation or their subordinate's motivational needs in order to help them reach their goals (Northouse, 2010). Leader behaviors along with task and follower characteristics are defined in detail in the following section.

**Terms:**

*Leader behaviors*

*Directive Leadership* – clear expectations made and communicated to followers

*Supportive Leadership* – create a pleasant work environment by treating followers as equals

*Participative Leadership* – leader and follower engaged in shared decision-making more democratic

*Achievement-Oriented Leadership* – challenge followers to work at their highest level (Northouse, 2010)

***Hindrances to high quality work from subordinates*** (Northouse, 2010)

*Unclear tasks* – leader needs to provide structure

*Highly repetitive tasks* – require more leadership support to maintain motivation

*Expectations unclear* – leader clarifies

*Roles (norms) unclear (weak)* – leader helps other understand role and builds unity

Subordinate Characteristics

| Subordinate Characteristic | Leadership Style Match |
|---|---|
| Needs for affiliation (feel good person) | Supportive Leadership |
| Believe they are in charge | Participative Leadership |
| Believe forces out of their control determine life | Directive Leadership |
| Need structure | Directive Leadership |
| Self-perceived low ability | Directive Leadership |
| Self-perceived high ability | Supportive, Participative, or Achievement-Oriented based on level of confidence and competence (see Situational Leadership) |

Source: Northouse, 2010, p. 129

**Implications:**

Know yourself, what you expect, and understand what your athletes/assistants/employees need to stay motivated.

When performing repetitive drills/tasks constantly provide support/encouragement.

Engage those you lead or lead with to see if you are communicating expectations clearly and clarify when needed.

Know your people to lead them with the best style.

When the team members understand their roles and a culture that aligns with those roles exists, they are more likely to stay motivated.

**Putting it in action:**

As part of the post-season/regular evaluation create a questionnaire like the Path-Goal Leadership Questionnaire to assess your perceived style and determine if this is the right match for your team.

In business determine which of the leadership behaviors is most appropriate for the project you are working on and the place you are in the project.

**Assessment Tool:**

*Path-Goal Leadership Questionnaire*

This assessment tool evaluates four different leadership areas to provide the leader with information on their strong and weak styles and the amount of importance they place on each style. This tool would help one see where he or she falls in relationship to directive, supportive, participative, and achievement-oriented styles (Northouse, 2010, p. 142).

Figure 6

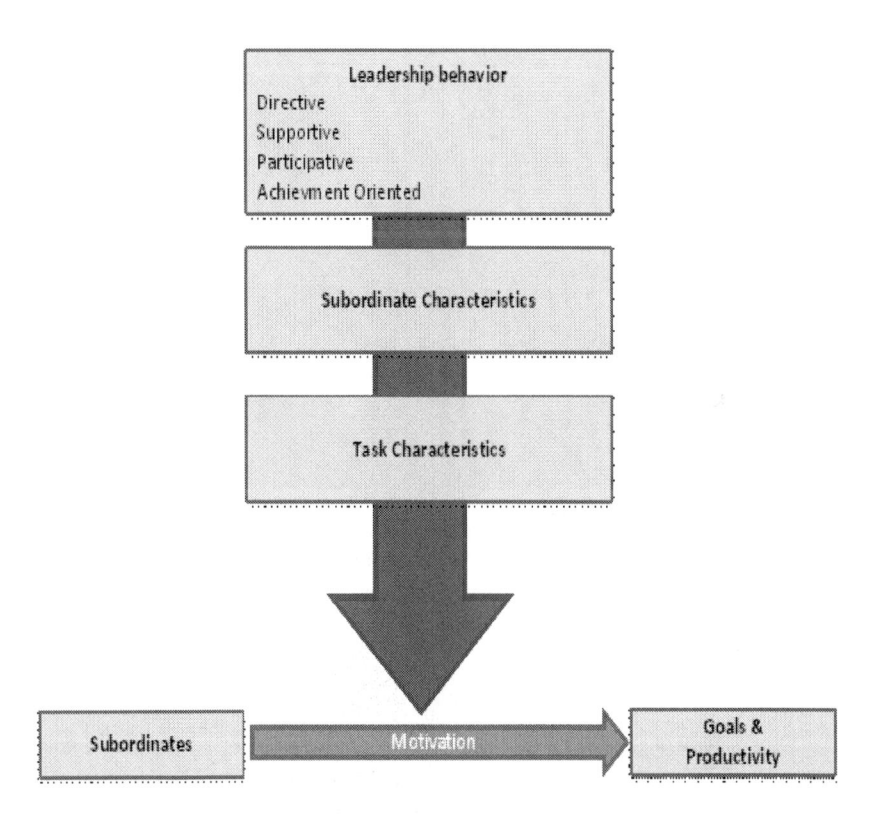

http://www.abolrous.com/hazem/images/Leadership/mhtABEB(1).png

# Leader-Member Exchange Theory

Have you been a part of an organization or team where you felt like you just did not belong? Maybe you felt there was a lot of "politics" on the team or in the organization. If you resonate with this then you have seen this theory in action in a negative way.

When beginning work with a team, group, or organization I have had to spend time building relationships. I was slow to understand this concept because of my results and task orientation. I now understand the value relationship building brings to a healthy organization.

Relational dynamics become unhealthy when "in groups" and "out groups" form. This creates a divided culture, but when the culture is healthy those who get results gain more trust with the leader. On the other hand, if people have a collaborative relationship with the leader primarily because of a special relationship, the organization will develop long term cultural problems.

This theory helps us look objectively at human interactions and raises our awareness of how to build a healthy culture of growth. Some people are content to maintain a specific relationship with the leader and do not want it to evolve while others like to see the relationship evolve. The leader's job is to help that relationship develop in a manner that creates and maintains a unified culture where progression is based both on trust and results.

**Definition:**

This theory looks at the process of interactions between the leader and his or her followers. At first this theory defined people as either "in" or "out" based on how much attention and extra responsibility they received from the leader (Northouse, 2010). (Figure 7) The better quality the relational exchanges between the leader and the follower, the less turnover in the organization.

More recently the theory of leadership making has evolved out of the desire for leaders to have a higher quality relationship with all members of the organization. Within this theory the leader/follower relationship progresses from stranger to acquaintance to partnership which is the phase with the most trust and respect (Northouse, 2010 referencing Graen & Uhl-Bien, 1991). Instead of creating a culture of in and out groups, leadership making attempts to create increased respect and trust among all members of the group (Northouse, 2010).

**Terms** (Northouse, 2010):

*Stranger* – the follower is driven by self-interest and follows orders from the leader

*Acquaintance* – follower has increased interest in the group's goal and starts to work more *with* instead of just *for* the leader

*Partner* – interdependence between follower and leader where leader shares his or her work load and follower may rely on the leader for more support

**Implications:**

Be aware of your leadership creating an "in-group" and "out-group". Be certain every member feels trusted, respected and valued in their role in order to prevent division within a team.

Take time after practices/meetings periodically to evaluate how you interact with those you lead. Determine if you are creating quality relationships on an equal level.

Be intentional about moving through the phases of leadership making so that your those you lead become some of your greatest champions for the team's vision. This process will multiply you and your efforts.

**Putting it in action:**

Just as a coach wants to be aware of how he or she communicates, the coach needs to be cognizant of the quality of his or her player/assistant relationships. Take time to talk with your players/assistants about more than just your sport. This can take you beyond the stranger and acquaintance phases into a more trusting partnership.

In business invest in those you lead to understand more about them than just their work to build trust in you as a person. Take the time to develop a relationship that will grow mutual trust.

**Assessment Tool:**

*LMX 7 Questionnaire*

A simple assessment tool to measure respect, trust and obligation and the overall quality of the exchanges between leaders and followers (Northouse, 2010). The results help one determine, from a respect and trust standpoint, the health of the leader and member relationship.

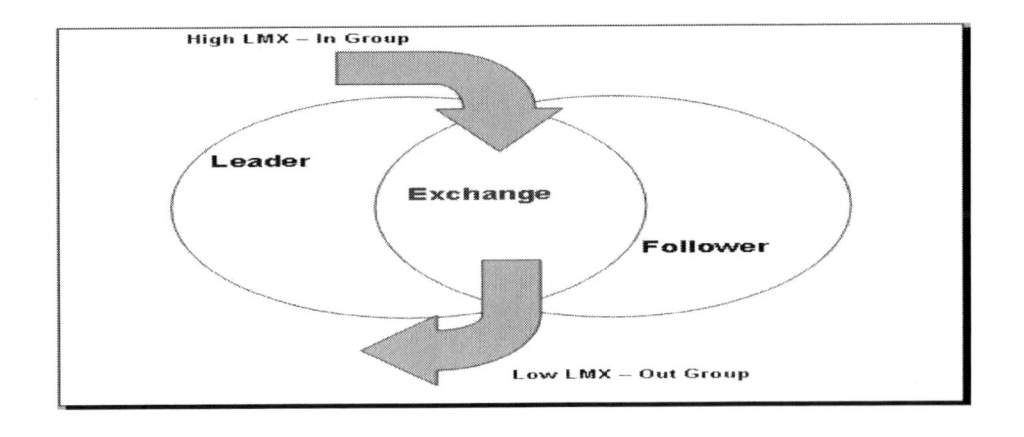

Figure 7

http://leadershipchamps.files.wordpress.com/2008/04/lmx-theory.jpg

# Transformational Leadership

In full disclosure this is one of my favorite theories. I have the opportunity to be part of a team of transformational leaders as a Maxwell Leadership certified executive program coach, trainer, and speaker. I seek to help people like you develop their leadership in a way that helps you transform your organization and the lives of those within it. John Maxwell's content helps people apply the ideas below in a practical way.

This leadership approach overflows from the heart of the leader and is informed by the leader's "why". You are the coach of a team, the leader of a business group, in a high level position in an organization, or have started your own company. . . . why? Ultimately why are you doing what you are doing?

In my first few years as a strength and conditioning coach I was busy trying to understand how to do what I was doing at a level to get results. Once I figured that out I began to ask myself, why am I doing this . . . really?

Yes, I wanted to help athletes get bigger, faster, and stronger in to reach their goals, but there was more. Ultimately, I wanted to use this environment to help athletes develop the discipline and responsibility required to meet a goal and help them become great leaders now and in the future. This "why" is what drove me throughout my career and possibly was a part of why I was able to experience success alongside some outstanding sport coaches.

As you read through this ask yourself "why?" Why are you really leading what you lead? What really drives you other than the money or the wins? When we understand this, we lead transformationally and make a real impact.

**Definition:**

This is a process of calling people to accomplish a greater goal through connecting with others' emotions and values to inspire a group toward action for a significant purpose. This process involves visionary and often charismatic leadership that is focused on the needs of others and not the leader's agenda (Northouse, 2010).

A charismatic leader demonstrates four key personality traits: a desire to influence, self-confidence, dominance, and strong moral values (Northouse, 2010). Transformational leadership is not limited to charisma and vision but began here and has developed over time by various people.

The opposite of this is *laissez-faire* leadership where the leader is uninvolved. Transactional leadership focuses on the exchanges or actions between leaders and followers. This approach is neither compelling like transformational nor uninvolved like *laissez-faire* leadership (Northouse, 2010). This is the "bossy" leader who people often want to quickly get away from.

Transformational leadership has four key factors: idealized influence/charisma, inspirational motivator, intellectually stimulating, individual consideration. Figure 8 pictures the "Full Range of Leadership Model" (Bass & Avolio, 1994) which illustrates the continuum of leadership from laissez-faire to transformational leadership and includes the various leadership factors from uninvolved through the various forms of transactional leadership to transformational leadership (Northouse, 2010). This model emphasizes the four "I's" of transformational leaders described by Bass and Avolio:

- Idealized influence/charisma
- Inspirational motivation
- Intellectual stimulation
- Individualized consideration (Northouse citing Bass & Avolio, 1994).

Bennis and Nanus (1985) and Kouzes and Posner (1987, 2002) describe two other forms of transformational leadership. Bennis and Nanus identified four strategies used by transformational leaders:

- They provide a clear vision
- They create a social culture of the organization
- They create trust
- They emphasize their strengths instead of focusing on weak areas.

Kouzes and Posner model of leadership describes five practices to be an exemplary leader.

- Model the way by being clear about the leader's values and philosophy.
- Create compelling visions or "inspire a shared vision."
- Challenge the process by being willing to create change and try new ideas.
- Enable others to act by creating a collaborative environment.
- Encourage the heart by rewarding others for what they have accomplished (Kouzes & Posner, 2002).

**Implications:**

To be a transformational coach/leader one must constantly remind his or her team of the big picture. Remind them of the ultimate goal and establish regular vision reminders with multiple methods: auditorily, visually, and kinesthetically.

Be innovative in how you approach leading so you can keep the vision fresh.

Learn from coaches/leaders around you and work together to create new ways to remind your team of the ultimate goal(s).

Analyze your approach to leadership from *laissez-fair* to transformational and adjust in ways that will best serve your team.

**Putting it in action:**

Create a visual reminder that keeps your team's overall goal and steps to accomplishing that goal in front of them.

Find the transformational leaders on your team and empower them to lead the team from their position.

Have a clear vision that is more than numbers driven, but life impacting and continually share it with your team.

**Assessment Tool:**

*Multifactor Leadership Questionnaire (MLQ)*

This tool provides a leader with information from his or her followers describing their perceptions of how the leader leads: involved, uninvolved, considerate, etc. This information will help a leader more clearly understand his or her leadership style as perceived by his or her followers and make changes where necessary.

Figure 8

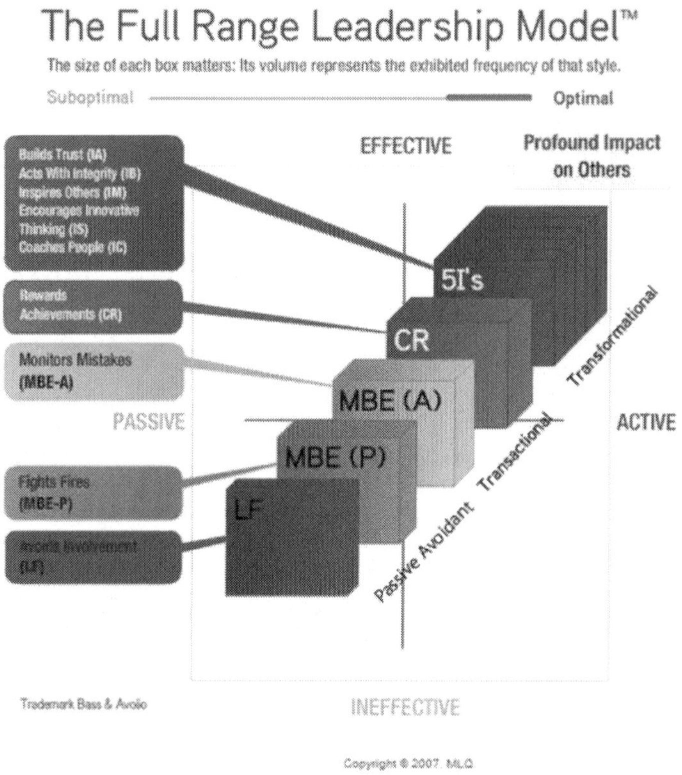

## The Full Range Leadership Model™

The size of each box matters: Its volume represents the exhibited frequency of that style.

http://www.mmurray.com.au/wp-content/uploads/2011/01/FRLM-Graphic.png

# Authentic Leadership

If you have read my book *25 Ways to Lead Better at Work and Home* or interacted with me through my blog or are on my e-mail list and get my weekly videos (go to www.wheelercoachingsystems.com to sign up) then you may sense this type of leadership is important to me. In a world that often shows the highlight reel many people simply want to know what is real. Let me clarify "real" by defining it as congruent. Do what I say and what I do match? Am I sincere about my failures as well as my successes?

There is a leader in my life who is appropriately transparent about what occurs within the organization and the person you see publicly matches who you see privately. She shares honestly and openly and as much as appropriate shares information openly with the entire team. This authenticity creates health and unity among the team.

When led by an authentic leader people are comfortable to offer their thoughts because the leader has the self-awareness and humility that they do not need to be the smartest person in the room. Authentic leaders are smart in many areas, but they welcome the value others in the group add. At the root of effective authentic leadership is humility and open-mindedness. Authentic leaders have a clear vision and are open to learning from those around them.

**Definition:**

Northouse (p. 217) suggests this is a relatively new theory with a developing definition. This theory shows the characteristics that create an authentic leader and what factors contribute to their development. Four components create an authentic leader:

- Balanced processing
- Self-awareness
- Relational transparency
- An internal moral perspective

As Figure 9 demonstrates the positive psychological traits of confidence, hope, optimism, and resilience combined with moral reasoning feed into critical life events that help develop the traits seen in an authentic leader. Two other individuals have contributed to developing the theory of authentic leadership. Robert Terry introduced the Authentic Action Wheel (Figure 10) which helps people diagnose and address organizational problems. An individual would find the problem on the middle of the wheel and then select the best response to the problem (Northouse, 2010, p.209).

Bill George provided character qualities of an authentic leader such as passion, compassion, behavior, connectedness, and consistency. These directly relate to the characteristics of purpose, heart, values, relationships, and self-discipline (Northouse, 2010).

**Terms:**

*Self-awareness* – a leader's personal insights

*Relational Transparency* – being honest/real in relationships with others

*Internal Moral Perspective* – internally determines moral standards instead of allowing outside pressures to influence them

*Balanced Processing* – analyzing information objectively and listening to others' opinions

**Implications:**

Transparency, especially when a mistake has been made, will raise your team's respect for you as the leader.

A leader who is aware will more likely respond logically instead of reacting on emotion.

This model is very relevant to younger generations who want those in authority to be genuine and consistent.

Practicing the element of balanced processing will help keep a coach/leader objective with his or her players when evaluating performance.

As the coach models this approach, assistants and players will learn and want to emulate this form of leadership if they have had a positive experience.

**Putting it in action:**

Next time you make a mistake, especially if you have unjustly blamed another, admit the mistake, and learn from it.

In business accept responsibility for your part in a failure even if a team member was primarily responsible.

**Assessment Tool:**

*Authentic Leadership Self-Assessment Questionnaire*

This tool is used to measure four areas of authentic leadership: internalized moral perspective, relational transparency, balanced processing and self-awareness

(Northouse, 2010, p. 235). The results help one understand certain measures such as their commitment to the organization and their satisfaction with their supervisors and their performance (Northouse, 2010).

Figure 9

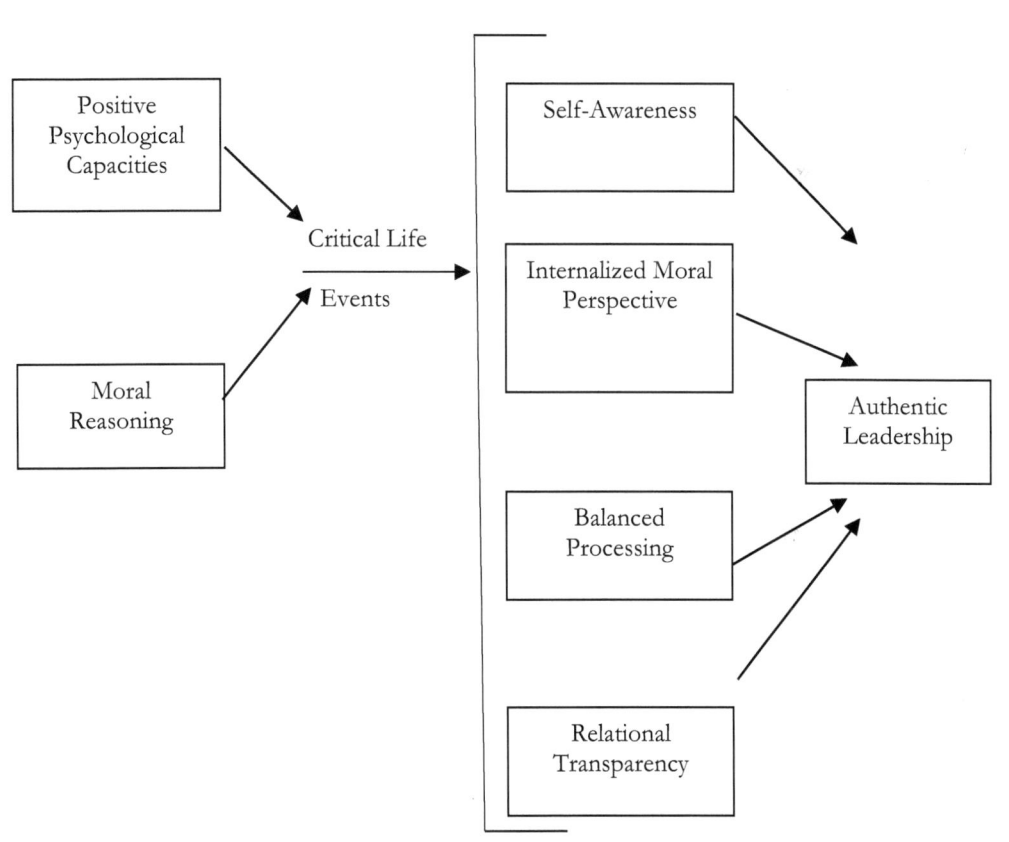

Source: Northouse, 2010, p. 217 citing Luthans, F. & Avolio, B.J. 2003. Authentic leadership development. In K.S. Cameron, J.E. Dutton, & R.E. Quinn (Eds.), *Positive organizational scholarship* (pp. 241-258). San Francisco: Berrett-Koehler, 2003; and W.L. Gardener, B.J. Avolio, F. Luthans, D.R. May, & F.O. Walumbwa, 2005. "Can you see the real me?" A self-based model of authentic leader and follower development. *Leadership Quarterly*, 16, 343-372.

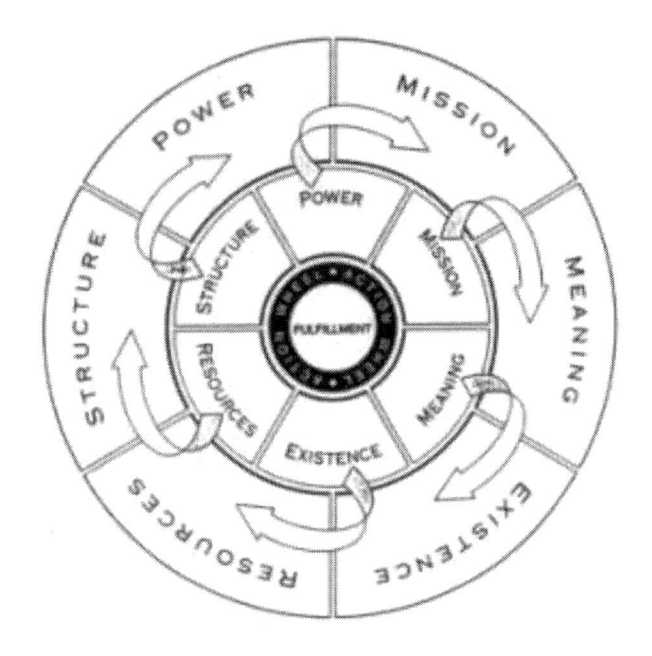

Source: *Authentic Leadership: Courage in Action*, by R. W. Terry. San Francisco: Jossey-Bass, 1993.
Reprinted with permission of the publishers. All rights reserved.

Figure 10

http://www.action-wheel.com/images/wheel2.jpg

# Team Leadership

Leading a team is a complex art. As when leading any group of individuals many dynamics come into play. I have had the opportunity to work alongside many sports coaches. Some have been quite successful to the point of leading their team to the ultimate championship while others have struggled.

Those coaches who have succeeded knew how to navigate the questions discussed in this theory in a successful manner. They may not have realized they were answering these questions, but as leaders they constantly evaluated their teams. Coaches and leaders navigate both individual and team dynamics to adjust either relationally or affect change for the culture of the team.

Problems are a part of leadership and this theory provides all leaders with a structure to look more objectively at the team related challenges they face. As you seek to lead your team create space to pause and reflect on the health of your group, team or organization. What, as the leader, are you responsible for in order to get improved results?

**Definition:**

This model addresses the leader's role as the overseer of a team. The leader's primary job is to help the group function effectively. Effective performance begins with the leader forming a model in their mind of the situation. This "mental model" is engaged to evaluate problems and find possible solutions while considering environmental and organizational restrictions and resources (Northouse, 2010 citing Zaccaro et al., 2001, p.462) .

A leader must first answer three key questions:

1. Should I monitor the team or take action?

2. Should I intervene to meet task or relational needs?

3. Should I intervene internally (conflict between members of the group) or externally (modify the environment)?

Figure 11 shows some of the actions the leader can take based on his or her answer to the three questions. The table below from Peter Northouse's findings describes the conditions of group effectiveness and characteristics of team excellence which will help a leader objectively assess his or her team (Northouse, 2010).

| Conditions of Group Effectiveness | Characteristics of Team Excellence |
|---|---|
| Clear, engaging direction<br>Enabling structure<br>Enabling context<br>Adequate material resources<br>Expert coaching | Clear, elevating goal<br>Results-driven structure<br>Competent team members<br>Unified commitment<br>Collaborative climate<br>Standards of excellence<br>External support and recognition<br>Principled leadership |

Source: Northouse, 2010 citing Hackman & Walton, 1986 and Larson & Lafasto, 1989

**Implications:**

This provides a tool for coaches/leaders to use in objectively assessing the needs of their team from the perspective of personnel interactions.

As the leader of the team, one needs to have a clear, engaging, and elevating goal.

Using this model to continually assess one's team will enable the coach to determine if past methods are effective or if they need to be changed/improved on.

**Putting it in action:**

Know the three primary questions and teach them to your assistants who can in turn teach them to their key athletes/leaders/employees.

**Assessment Tool:**

*Team Excellence and Collaborative Team Leader Questionnaire*

This instrument evaluates eight factors that determine a team's performance level and the results help the leader determine the areas that need corrective action (Northouse, 2010, p. 265). Both the team members and leaders take the assessment and compare the results. The team then finds weak areas and makes necessary changes. This is designed to "help teams sort through the complex problems confronting them and to pinpoint areas for action" (Northouse, 2010, p.265).

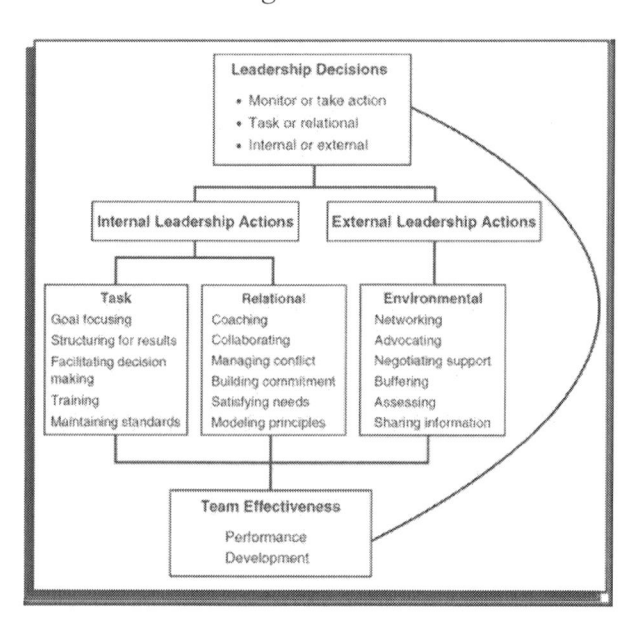

Figure 11

http://2.bp.blogspot.com/_SA1TmgxioB4/TM78aWUliMI/AAAAAAAAAc/mEOReBRt6v0/s1600/leadership+pic+2.jpg

# Psychodynamic Approach

At times when I work with organizations I help them understand the interpersonal dynamics of relationships through utilizing the DISC based Maxwell Personality Indicator Reports. Think of someone who drives you nuts either personally or professionally. Now before you go down the rabbit hole too far, could it be possible you are frustrated because you do not *understand* that person?

At times our conflict is because of habits and we either need to address or accept that person's habits. Other times the challenge comes out of not understanding another person's personality and how it affects their thinking and behavior. We can all change and grow but understanding our basic personality and that of those we work alongside can improve team dynamics drastically.

In this section we will dive deep into one specific personality indicator, but if you want to learn more contact me and I would love to help you and your team.

**Definition:**

This theory approaches leadership trying to understand the personality of both the leader and his or her subordinates (Northouse, 2010). This approach ultimately seeks to provide clarity in understanding the leader/follower relationship. It suggests various personalities are better suited for certain leadership situations than others.

Effective leadership requires an awareness of transactions between the leader and follower as shown in Figure 12. People work best when they both interact from the adult ego state. Multiple theorists have influenced this approach from Freud and his ego states to Eric Fromm, and most recently Michael Maccoby who described the productive narcissist or the driven self-focused leader who fails to consider how his or her pursuit may impact those around him or her (Northouse citing Maccoby, 2003, p.86).

Carl Jung has provided the basis for a commonly used personality test: the Myers-Briggs Type Indicator. The four dimensions he explained are illustrated in Figure 13. His contribution provides a wide variety of personality types to help a leader understand him or herself better as well as his or her subordinates (Northouse, 2010).

**Terms** (Northouse, 2010):

*Introversion* – listeners, energized by being alone

*Extroversion* – talkers, gets energy from outside him or her self

*Sensing* – gather information through senses, factual and practical

*Intuition* – abstract and dreamers

*Thinking* – objective, analytical and logical

*Feeling* – consider other's feelings and peacekeepers

*Judging* – structured, deliberate, plan-oriented

*Perceiving* – spontaneous, flexible, and more easy-going

**Implications:**

Understanding your staff member's or team member's personalities will help you to effectively adapt your responses and motivational techniques.

Be aware of whether you respond from an adult, parent or child state when working with your staff or players.

Invest in understanding your own personality to see if you are in the best role suited for your personality type.

**Putting it in action:**

Invest in the DISC based Maxwell Personality Indicator to understand various facets of individual personality and leadership strengths and how their behavior impacts others on your team. (http://bit.ly/2HHaX5S)

Invest in the MBTI test to have your athletes/team members take or create a simplified version to help you understand where your athletes/team fall in the four dimensions Jung described.

*(As an aside: I find the DISC tool to be easier to understand and implement to improve team culture and communication than other tools.)*

**Assessment Tools:**

*Psychodynamic Approach Survey*

A shortened version of the MBTI that helps one quickly determine their personality type (Northouse, 2010).

*Myers/Briggs (MBTI)*

A detailed analysis of where one falls on the eight personality preferences. The four preferences form one's personality type. Understanding one's type will help a leader understand how their personality fits with others on their team and with the role he or she is expected to fulfill (Northouse, 2010).

*DISC Based Assessments*

An assessment that helps individuals understand their basic personality tendencies and how they interact in a group environment. MBTI helps understand how people think internally while DISC helps one understand how personality relates to external behaviors and is easier to apply in group settings.

Figure 12

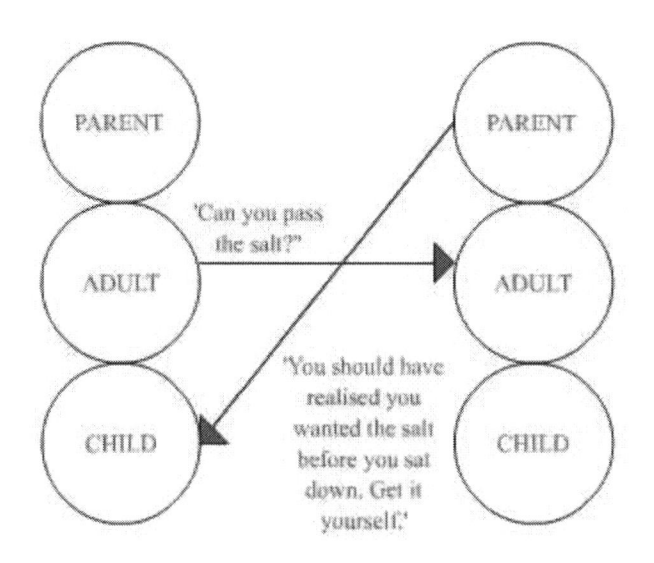

http://www.uktherapy.info/images/T2.jpg

Figure 13

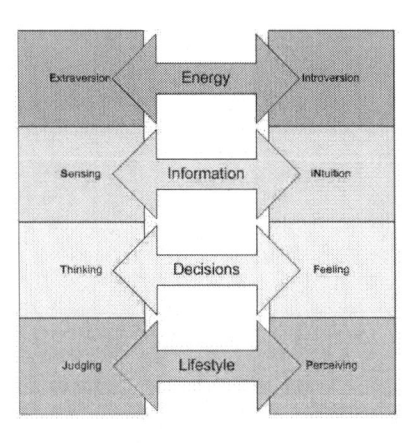

http://corejolts.files.wordpress.com/2011/02/mbti-dichotomies-blank-background.jpg

Conclusion

I hope as you have read through this resource you have found it helpful and practical. My hope is that you periodically return to this to reflect on your leadership and how you can continue to grow and develop as a leader. Theory is good, but now is the time when you must put this into action.

I encourage you to go back to the theory you most resonated with and dig a little deeper into it. Think into how you can grow in that area as a leader. Think into how you can help develop other leaders. As leaders we can develop followers who simply do what we say or leaders who will carry the vision on when we are gone. Which do you want to develop?

Thank you for investing your time to read this. If you have found it valuable feel free to share with me what you got out of this book and tell others. In the meantime, lead well in all you do.

Randy Wheeler

randy@wheelercoachingsystems.com

Go to: https://www.wheelercoachingsystems.com/ for a free leadership ebook

317.523.5977

References

Bass, B. M., & Avolio, B.J. (1994). *Improving organizational effectiveness through transformational leadership.* Thousand Oakes, CA: Sage.

Bennis, W. G., & Nanus, B. (1985). *Leaders: The strategies for taking charge.* New York: Harper and Row.

Blake, R.R., & McCanse, A. A. (1991). *Leadership dilemnas: Grid solutions.* Houston, TX: Gulf Publishing Company.

Blanchard, K. Zigarmi, P. & Zigarmi, D. (1985). *Leadership and the one minute manager: Increasing effectiveness through situational leadership.* New York: William Morrow.

Fiedler, F. E. (1967). *A theory of leadership effectiveness.* New York: McGraw-Hill.

Gardener, W. L.., Avolio, B.J., Luthans, F. May, D.R. & Walumbwa, F.O. 2005. "Can you see the real me?" A self-based model of authentic leader and follower development. *Leadership Quarterly,* 16, 343-372.

Goleman, D. (1995). *Emotional intelligence.* New York: Bantam.

Graen, G.B. & Uhl-Bien, M. (1991). The transformation of professionals into self-managing and partially self-designing contributions: Toward a theory of leadership making. *Journal of Management System*s, 3(3), 33-48.

Hackman, J.R., & Walton, R.E. (1986). Leading groups in organizations. In P.S. Goodman & Associates (Eds.), *Designing effective work groups* (pp. 72-119). San Francisco: Jossey-Bass.

Judge, T.A., Bono, J.E. Ilies, R., & Gerhardt, M.W. (2002). Personality and leadership: A qualitative and quantitative review. *Journal of Applied Psychology,* 87, 765-780.

Katz, R. L. (1955). Skills of an effective administrator. *Harvard Business Review,* 33(1), 33-42.

Kirkpatrick, S.A., & Locke, E. A. (1991). Leadership: Do traits matter? *The Executive,* 5, 48-60.

Kouzes, J.M., & Posner, B.Z. (1987). *The leadership challenge: How to get extraordinary things done in organizations.* San Franciso: Jossey-Bass.

Kouzes, J.M., & Posner, B.Z. (2002). *The leadership challenge* (3rd ed.). San Francisco: Jossey-Bass.

Larson, C.E., & LaFasto, F.M.J. (1989). *Teamwork: What must go right/what can go wrong.* Newbury Park, CA:Sage.

Luthans, F. & Avolio, B.J. 2003. Authentic leadership development. In K.S. Cameron, J.E. Dutton, & R.E. Quinn (Eds.), *Positive organizational scholarship* (pp. 241-258). San Francisco: Berrett-Koehler, 2003.

Maccoby, M. (2003). *The productive narcissist: The promise and peril of visionary leadership.* New York: Broadway

Mumford, M. D., Zaccaro, S. J., Harding, F. D., Jacobs, T. O., & Fleishman, E. A. (2000).

Leadership skills for a changing world: Solving complex social problems. *Leadership Quarterly*, 11(1), 11-35.

Northouse, P. (2010). *Leadership: theory and practice.* (5 ed., pp. 69 -78). Los Angeles: SAGE.

Stogdill, R.M. (1948). Personal factors associated with leadership: A survey of the literature. *Journal of Psychology,* 25, 35-71.

Stogdill, R. M. (1974). *Handbook of leadership: A survey of theory and research.* New York: Free Press.

Stogdill, R. M. (1963). *Manual for the Leader Behavior Description Questionnaire form XII.* Columbus: Ohio State University, Bureau of Business Research.

Zacarro, S. J., Rittman, A.L., & Marks, M.A. (2001). Team leadership. *Leadership Quarterly*, 12, 451-483.

# Additional Leadership Resources

### *Books by Coaches on Leadership*

*Wooden on Leadership* John Wooden and Steve Jamison

*Success Is A Choice* Rick Pitino with Bill Reynolds

*Winning Every Day* Lou Holtz

*The Bowden Way* Bobby Bowden

*Leading With the Heart* Mike Krzyzewski

### *Books related to theories mentioned and other related books*

*On Becoming a Leader* Warren Bennis

*Primal Leadership* Daniel Goleman

*Good to Great* Jim Collins

*True North* Bill George (practical application of authentic leadership)

*Authentic Leadership* Bill George

*Self-Leadership and the One Minute Manager* Ken Blanchard

*Lincoln on Leadership* Donald T. Phillips

*The 21 Irrefutable Laws of Leadership* John Maxwell (practical application of transformational leadership)

Made in the USA
Columbia, SC
17 August 2022